# ON THE HUNT WITH

# WOLVES

## SANDRA MARKLE

Lerner Publications ◆ Minneapolis

# THE ANIMAL WORLD IS FULL OF PREDATORS.

Predators are the hunters that find, catch, and eat other animals—their prey—in order to survive. Every environment has its chain of hunters. The smaller, slower, less able predators become part of the prey for the bigger, faster, more cunning hunters. And everywhere, there are just a few kinds of predators at the top of the food chain. These are the top predators. Across the treeless Arctic and the forests, prairies, grasslands, and even swamps of North America, Europe, Asia, and North Africa, the top predators include wolves. Scientists debate how many species (kinds) of wolves there are. But everyone agrees the largest of these top predators is the gray wolf.

Why are gray wolves one of the top predators? For one thing, the adults are big enough to bring down their habitat's biggest prey, such as elk, moose, and bison. These prey animals are much bigger than gray wolves. So the wolves usually hunt them as a group—a wolf pack. Some large, adult gray wolves, however, can overpower big prey on their own. By the time a male gray wolf is three years old and full-grown, he's usually 6 feet (1.8 m) long from nose to tail tip. He weighs about 115 pounds (52 kg).

Female gray wolves are smaller and weigh less than males. But just like males, they are strong and built for chasing down prey.

**WOW!**
**A gray wolf can cover 12 feet (3.6 m) in one leap!**

Another reason gray wolves are top predators is they can run nonstop for long distances. Although a wolf only walks and runs on its toes, it has rough toe pads and thick, blunt claws that keep it from slipping. Scientists have observed wolves trotting over 30 miles (48 km) in a day while searching for prey. Gray wolves also chase prey to make it tired enough to slow down. Then the pack can surround and close in on its target.

Another reason a gray wolf is a top predator is its keen senses. The sense it counts on most is smell. A wolf can detect the scent of prey, such as a moose, from a mile (1.6 km) away.

A wolf's hearing is sharp too. Gray wolves start moving toward prey sounds they hear from as far away as 6 miles (9.6 km) in forested areas. They hear sounds up to 10 miles (16 km) across open fields. A wolf hears so well because the big ears on top of its head are sound scoops. When it detects possible prey noises, a wolf turns its ears separately to the left and right. That's how it tells where the noises are loudest so it can home in on their source.

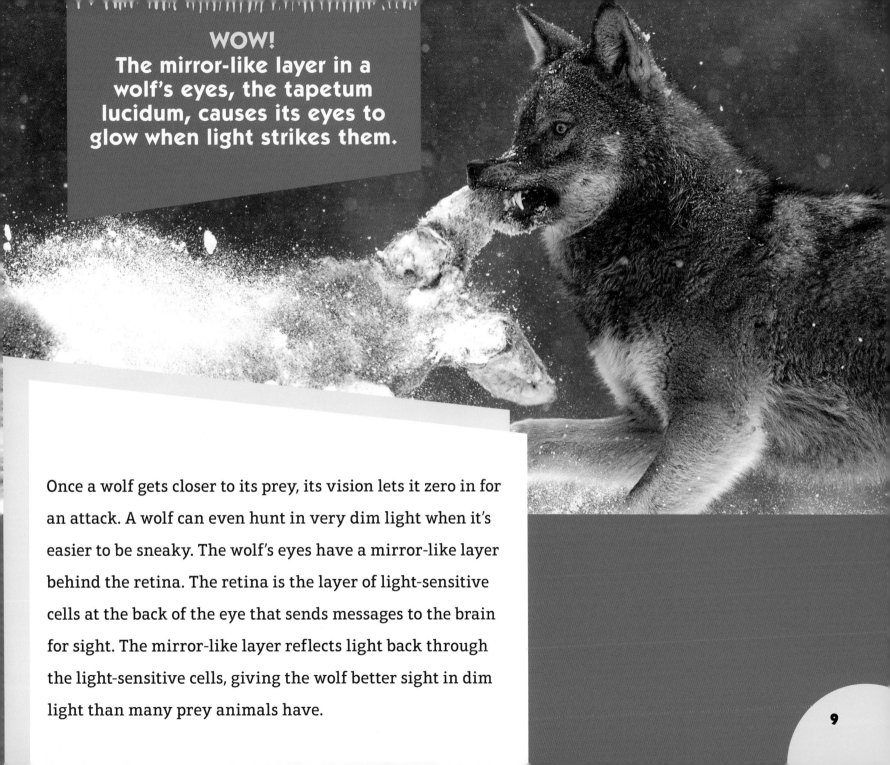

**WOW!**
The mirror-like layer in a wolf's eyes, the tapetum lucidum, causes its eyes to glow when light strikes them.

Once a wolf gets closer to its prey, its vision lets it zero in for an attack. A wolf can even hunt in very dim light when it's easier to be sneaky. The wolf's eyes have a mirror-like layer behind the retina. The retina is the layer of light-sensitive cells at the back of the eye that sends messages to the brain for sight. The mirror-like layer reflects light back through the light-sensitive cells, giving the wolf better sight in dim light than many prey animals have.

9

Yet another reason a gray wolf is a top predator is its bite. And what a weapon it is! When a wolf bites its prey, the wolf's largest teeth (canines) interlock. That helps make its bite force strong enough to break bones.

**WOW!**
An adult wolf has forty-two teeth—ten more than an adult human has.

Once its prey is killed, a wolf nips open the skin with its small front teeth (incisors). It also bites to rip off chunks of meat. The wolf's back teeth (molars) crush its food, including bones. The fatty marrow inside bones is high-energy food for wolves.

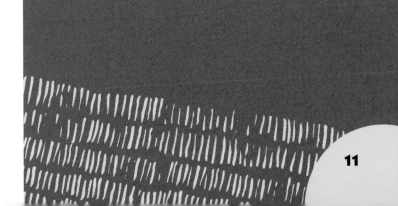

But the number one reason a gray wolf is a top predator is that it hunts with a team—its pack. The pack may be just a pair of wolves, a male and a female, or it may be a large group. But the pack is always a family starting with the parents, which are often called the alpha male and alpha female. It also includes any pups they have plus brothers and sisters of previous alphas. Sometimes, a few unrelated wolves are allowed to join the pack.

When a pack goes hunting, it usually takes at least four wolves to bring down large prey, such as elk. A pack of at least eleven wolves is needed for hunting the biggest prey, such as bison. More wolves may go along on hunts, but some always hang back to avoid risk of injury. After all, most prey fight back.

This time the pack's prey is a moose whose big ears and large eyes have alerted it to the approaching wolves. The moose runs away as the pack closes in.

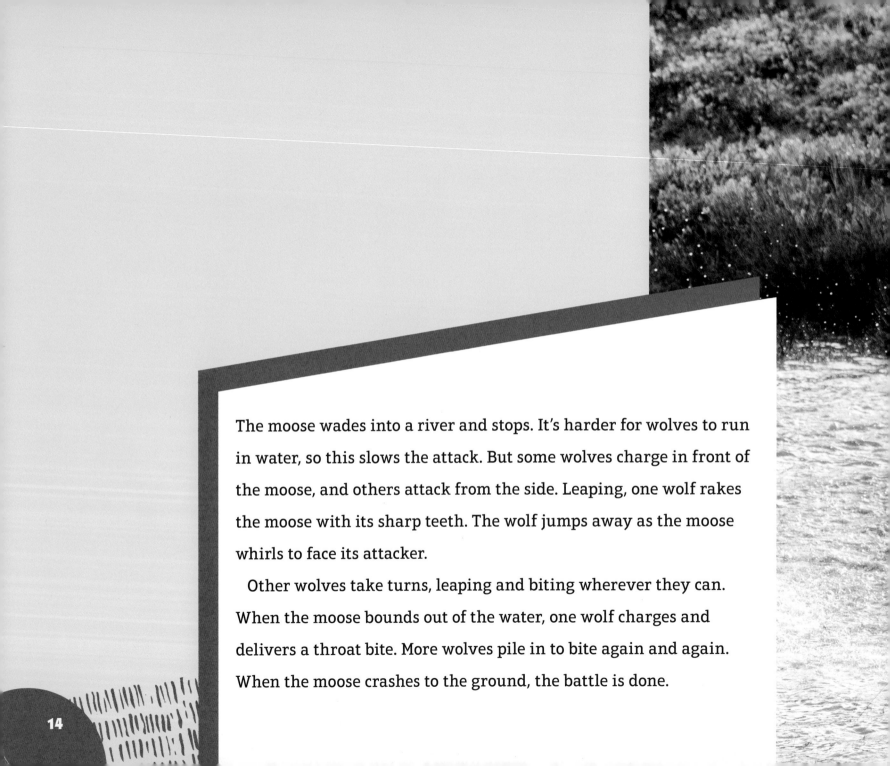

The moose wades into a river and stops. It's harder for wolves to run in water, so this slows the attack. But some wolves charge in front of the moose, and others attack from the side. Leaping, one wolf rakes the moose with its sharp teeth. The wolf jumps away as the moose whirls to face its attacker.

Other wolves take turns, leaping and biting wherever they can. When the moose bounds out of the water, one wolf charges and delivers a throat bite. More wolves pile in to bite again and again. When the moose crashes to the ground, the battle is done.

**WOW!**
A wolf may eat up to 22 pounds
(10 kg) of meat in one meal.

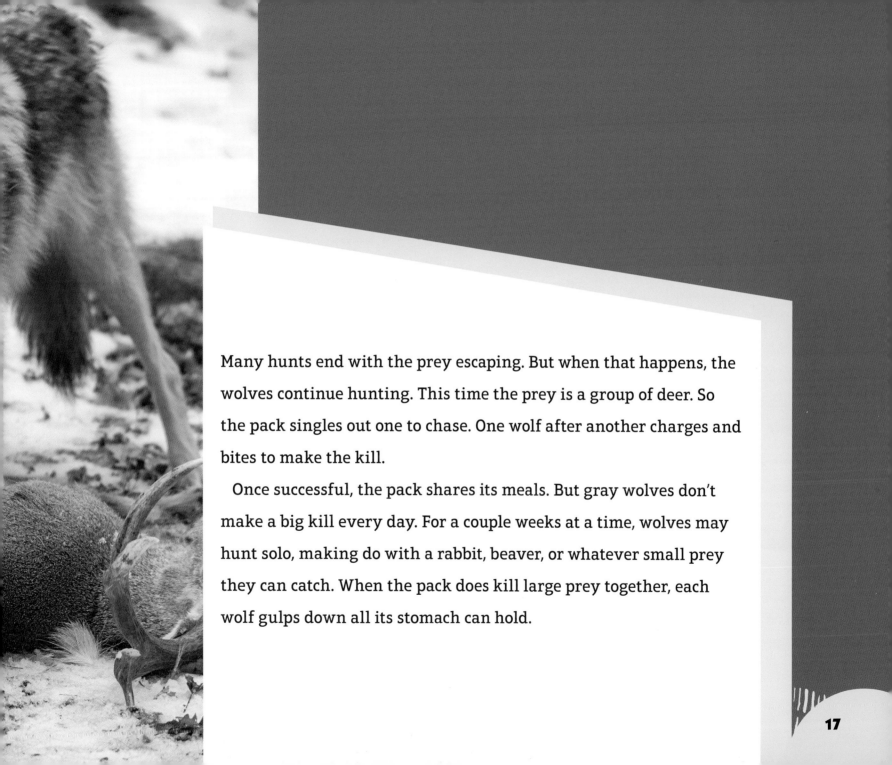

Many hunts end with the prey escaping. But when that happens, the wolves continue hunting. This time the prey is a group of deer. So the pack singles out one to chase. One wolf after another charges and bites to make the kill.

Once successful, the pack shares its meals. But gray wolves don't make a big kill every day. For a couple weeks at a time, wolves may hunt solo, making do with a rabbit, beaver, or whatever small prey they can catch. When the pack does kill large prey together, each wolf gulps down all its stomach can hold.

After a big meal, the wolves curl up and sleep. This rest is a good way to give their bodies time to digest. It also gives them energy for playing.

Full of energy, the wolves chase one another and play fight. It's partly fun and partly team building. Playing also maintains pack rank. Adults dominate youngsters, and stronger adults dominate weaker ones. Pack members show submission by crouching and licking the more dominant wolf's nose and mouth.

**WOW!**
In open country, a wolf's howl can be heard 10 miles (16 km) away.

A gray wolf pack stays connected by howling together. The alpha male or alpha female leads off, and the others join in. Or a wolf may howl to gain its pack's support. For example, a wolf hunting small prey by itself might spot bigger prey and howl to call the pack for a group hunt. A solo hunter might also howl to warn the pack of danger. Despite being top predators, wolves have their own predators, including grizzly bears and humans.

Gray wolves also howl to tell any nearby roaming wolves the area is already claimed. The pack's territory is critical to its survival. It's an area the wolves can count on for prey and water without having to travel long distances. It also includes a sheltered spot where the alpha female can safely give birth.

Wolves mate during the winter, and babies develop inside the female's body for about sixty-seven days. In late April or early May, the mother gives birth to between one and eleven pups. At first, the youngsters are small and toothless. Their eyes are sealed shut, and they have too little hair to stay warm. So the pups snuggle against their mother and nurse often as they continue to develop. Meanwhile, the pack keeps hunting and carries food home for the new mother.

At just three weeks old, the pack's future hunters can see, have their baby teeth, and are furry balls of energy. Then their mother takes them to meet the pack. Although usually only the alpha pair produce pups, once out of the den, the entire pack helps guard, raise, and train the youngsters.

## WOW!
A wolf kills with its bite, but it can also carry a pup in its mouth so gently that its teeth never prick the youngster's skin.

While another pack member pup-sits, the alpha
female returns to hunting. As one of the pack's
strongest members, she helps the pack make kills.
Hunting also lets the mother eat her fill. Back with
her family, the pups lick their
mother's mouth. That triggers
her to bring up some of her
partly digested meal for the
pups to eat. As they get bigger,
the pups also beg and receive
food from other wolves. This
way the pups begin to eat solid
food, though they continue
to nurse until they are about
nine weeks old.

Wolf pups have toys, like a piece of fur from a prey animal. The pups sink their baby teeth into the soft skin, getting a taste of what they will one day hunt. When several pups wrestle for a toy, the winner runs away with its prize. But victory only lasts until the other pups catch up. Then the youngsters wrestle again.

Day after day, the pups do a lot of play fighting. This helps them grow stronger. Play fighting is also how they begin to learn about proving dominance in the group.

The pups are hunters-in-training. At first, they chase bugs, field mice, and fish they spy swimming close to a river's edge. Both hunting failures and successes are valuable lessons.

While learning how to hunt, the pups are also becoming young adults. Their coats change from puppy fuzz to an adult's double coat: underhair traps body heat, and outer guard hair sheds water and snow. Their legs grow longer too, preparing them for long-distance chases and leaps. They also get bigger, stronger adult teeth.

Young wolves are nearly full-grown by winter.
Though still trainees, they hunt with the pack,
developing their skills and learning their territory.

By the time new pups are born in the spring, the
young adult gray wolves are effective hunters. They'll
pup-sit and help train the newest members of this top
predator's family pack.

# A NOTE FROM SANDRA MARKLE

**Even top predators face risks,** and a global change in Earth's climate is challenging gray wolves. Scientists measure the Arctic region—home to most gray wolves—warming at a faster rate than anywhere else on Earth. This affects gray wolves by changing conditions for the prey animals they depend on.

Rising temperatures mean less snow during the winter, earlier snowmelt in spring, and water shortage in late summer. That affects the plants that prey animals, such as deer, need for food. Warming also allows plant diseases to spread more easily, decreasing the food supply for the wolf's prey even more. Although the pack might continue to get by, without enough food, alpha females may not produce pups. If that happens, pack sizes will decrease, and over time, some packs will even cease to exist.

Photo by Skip Jeffery Photography

# GRAY WOLF SNAP FACTS

## ADULT SIZE

Males are larger than females. Males may be 6 feet (1.8 m) long and weigh up to 115 pounds (52 kg).

## DIET

They only eat animals, including rabbits, mice, and large prey such as deer, elk, moose, and bison.

## RANGE

They are found mainly in the wilderness and remote areas of Canada, Alaska, the northern United States, Europe, and Asia.

## FUN FACT

A pack's top-ranking alpha male and alpha female are easy to spot because they approach other pack members with their tails held high.

## LIFE SPAN

In the wild, they live as long as thirteen years.

## YOUNG

Females give birth to between one and eleven pups after they develop inside her for about sixty-seven days.

# GLOSSARY

**ALPHA:** the strongest, dominant male or female wolf that leads a pack. The alpha male and alpha female are usually the only pair to mate and produce pups.

**DEN:** a home, such as a burrow or a cave, where the alpha female wolf gives birth to her pups

**FOOD CHAIN:** a series of living things where each is dependent on another as a source of food

**NURSE:** to feed on milk from a mother's body

**PREDATOR:** an animal that hunts and eats other animals

**PREY:** an animal that a predator catches to eat

**PUP:** a baby wolf

**TERRITORY:** an area where a wolf pack usually hunts. A wolf pack will defend its territory against other wolves.

# INDEX

Image credits: blickwinkel/Alamy Stock Photo, pp. 2-3, 9; Marco Arduino/Alamy Stock Photo, p. 4; Stock Connection Blue/Alamy Stock Photo, p. 5; Ben Queenborough/Alamy Stock Photo, pp. 6-7; MikhailSemenov/iStock/Getty Images, p. 8; Nicolette Wollentin/iStock/Getty Images, p. 10; Cindy Hopkins/Alamy Stock Photo, p. 11; Chase Swift/Getty Images, pp. 12 -13; Patrick J. Endres/Getty Images, p. 15; Holly Kuchera/Alamy Stock Photo, pp. 16 -17; Arterra Picture Library/Alamy Stock Photo, p. 18; Winfried Schäfer/Alamy Stock Photo, p. 19; Roberto Gonzalez/Alamy Stock Photo, pp. 20-21; Westend61/Getty Images, p. 22; Picture by Tambako the Jaguar/Getty Images, p. 23; slowmotiongli/Getty Images, p. 24; Design Pics Inc/Alamy Stock Photo, p. 25; Nature Picture Library/Alamy Stock Photo, p. 26; Arterra Picture Library/Alamy Stock Photo, p. 27.

Cover: Wolfgang Kaehler/LightRocket/Getty Images.

THE AUTHOR WOULD LIKE TO THANK DR. DANIEL MACNULTY, UTAH STATE UNIVERSITY, LOGAN, UTAH, AND DR. DOUGLAS SMITH, PROJECT LEADER, WOLF RESTORATION PROJECT, YELLOWSTONE NATIONAL PARK, FOR SHARING THEIR ENTHUSIASM AND EXPERTISE.

A SPECIAL THANK-YOU TO SKIP JEFFERY FOR HIS LOVING SUPPORT DURING THE CREATIVE PROCESS.

FOR JESSICA GROEBE AND ALL THE CHILDREN AT INDEPENDENCE ELEMENTARY SCHOOL IN BOLINGBROOK, ILLINOIS

Lerner Publications Company
An imprint of Lerner Publishing Group, Inc.
241 First Avenue North
Minneapolis, MN 55401 USA

For reading levels and more information, look up this title at www.lernerbooks.com.

Main body text set in Aptifer Slab LT Pro medium.
Typeface provided by Linotype AG.

**Library of Congress Cataloging-in-Publication Data**

Names: Markle, Sandra, author.
Title: On the hunt with wolves / Sandra Markle.
Description: Minneapolis, MN : Lerner Publications, [2023] | Series: Ultimate predators | Includes index. | Audience: Ages 8–12 | Audience: Grades 4–6 | Summary: "With their sharp senses, ability to run long distances, and powerful bites, wolves are top predators in their habitats. Find out how they work together to hunt and raise their young"— Provided by publisher.
Identifiers: LCCN 2021056745 (print) | LCCN 2021056746 (ebook) | ISBN 9781728456263 (library binding) | ISBN 9781728464442 (paperback) | ISBN 9781728462479 (ebook)
Subjects: LCSH: Wolves—Juvenile literature. | Predatory animals—Juvenile literature.
Classification: LCC QL737.C22 M3637 2023  (print) | LCC QL737.C22  (ebook) | DDC 599.773—dc23/eng/20211122

LC record available at https://lccn.loc.gov/2021056745
LC ebook record available at https://lccn.loc.gov/2021056746

Manufactured in the United States of America
1-50696-50115-3/8/2022